What

Would

You Be?

By Wyatt Michaels

Copyright 2012

Image courtesy of dingopup

What would you be if you traveled in space?

    A. Architect

    B. Astronaut

    C. Space chimp

Image courtesy of tami.vroma

The answer is B. Astronaut

Becoming an astronaut isn't easy but it is worth it if it is something you really want to do.

Some buildings that are designed by an architect may be so tall that they feel like they are in space!

Chimps have traveled in space but being one is not an option for you.

What would you be if you rode in a big shiny red truck? (But the truck wouldn't look like this one.)

A. Fireman
B. Pilot
C. Policeman

Image courtesy of Sean McGinnis

The answer is   A. Fireman

Not all fire trucks are red, but they are big and usually kept very shiny.

Pilots fly airplanes instead of drive trucks.

Policemen can work with those who drive the big red trucks, but they don't usually drive them.

Image courtesy of Mosman Council

What would you be if you helped pets be healthy?

A. Banker
B. Paramedic
C. Veterinarian

Image courtesy of Tobyotter

The answer is C. Veterinarian

It's a big word for a very important job.

Bankers work with money instead of pets.

Paramedics help get people, not pets, to the hospital.

Image courtesy of woodleywonderworks

What would you be if you grew crops so other people would have food?

    A. Farmer
    B. Grocer
    C. Waitress

Image courtesy of US Embassy New Zealand

The answer is A. Farmer

Farmers work hard to make sure there is food available for everyone.

Grocers sell food in grocery stores, but somebody else grows the food.

Waitresses bring food to your table in a restaurant, but they don't grow the crops from which the food is made.

Image courtesy of stan

What would you be if you delivered products to stores?

    A. Plumber
    B. Taxi Driver
    C. Truck Driver

Image courtesy of Lady Dragonfly CC

The answer is C. Truck Driver

Truck drivers deliver lots of things to lots of places, including the things that you buy from a store.

Plumbers work on pipes that carry water to and from your house.

Taxi drivers deliver people to where they want to go, but they don't usually deliver products to stores.

Image courtesy of Marc van der Chijs

What would you be if you helped people get well?

A. Coach

B. Mailman

C. Nurse

The answer is C. Nurse

Nurses work in many different places, but they do their work so that you can be healthy.

Coaches help people do better in many different sports.

Mailmen deliver mail to your mailbox.

Image courtesy of Editor B

What would you be if you helped kids and adults learn about things?

- A. Beautician
- B. Teacher
- C. Flight Attendant

Image courtesy of myfuture.com

The answer is B. Teacher

Teachers can be in many different places. Wherever they are, they help kids or adults learn something new.

Beauticians help your hair look beautiful.

Flight attendants help you know what to do on an airplane, but that's about all the teaching they do.

Image courtesy of Infrogmation

What would you be if you told others about things that are happening?

A. Electrician
B. Reporter
C. Teller

Image courtesy of Damian Kettlewell for council in West Vancouver

The answer is B. Reporter

Reporters gather information and then report the news on tv, radio, or on the internet.

Electricians know how to run wires so your lights, refrigerator, and computer will have the power they need to be on.

You would think that a teller "tells" something, right? But a teller is the person at the bank that helps you with your money.

Image courtesy of Corey Ann

What would you be if you helped others know what the weather might be like?

A. Chef
B. Football Player
C. Meteorologist

Image courtesy of Kazz 0

The answer is C. Meteorologist

Meteorologist is a big word that means "someone who studies the weather".

Chefs work around food instead of studying weather.

Football players probably want to know what the weather will be like for their game, but they don't try to predict what it will be.

Image courtesy of Photo Dudes

What would you be if you moved dirt to make roads or buildings?

    A. Engineer
    B. Heavy Equipment Operator
    C. Landscaper

Image courtesy of Photo Dudes

The answer is B. Heavy Equipment Operator

Bulldozers, cranes, and other big machinery are run by heavy equipment operators.

Even though an engineer has the word "engine" in his name, he doesn't drive big equipment.

Landscapers move dirt, but not as much as someone else does.

Image courtesy of esivesind

What would you be if you told people about God in church?

A. Author
B. Draftsman
C. Preacher

Image courtesy of amish steve

The answer is   C. Preacher

Preachers are usually in churches when they teach people about God. Sometimes they are called a pastor.

Authors can tell people about God through their books, but they don't usually stand in front of people in a church.

Draftsmen draw the plans so people will know how to build a building.

Image courtesy of public domain

What would you be if you got things out of the ground for people to use?

A. Accountant
B. Garbage Collector
C. Miner

Image courtesy of woodleywonderworks

The answer is A. Miner

Miners can mine for many different valuables including gold, coal, silver, and other precious metals.

Garbage collectors have a dirty job, but someone else works in the dirt.

Accountants like to work with numbers instead of rocks and dirt.

Image courtesy of InfoMofo

What would you be if you made doughnuts, cakes, or breads?

A. Air Traffic Controller
B. Baker
C. Cabinet Maker

The answer is B. Baker

A baker also bakes cookies, muffins, and pies.

Air Traffic Controllers direct pilots at busy airports so they know when to land their airplane.

Cabinet makers make cabinets that are used by the person who makes doughnuts, cakes, and breads.

Image courtesy of Michael Cory

What would you be if you helped keep our roads and cities safe?

A. Actor
B. Doctor
C. Policeman

Image courtesy of Peter J Bellis

The answer is C. Policeman

Police men and women work hard to keep our communities safe.

Actors keep our roads and cities safe only in the movies!

Doctors help people feel better.

Image courtesy of dennis tang

What would you be if you sang or played instruments for people to enjoy?

A. Baseball player
B. Musician
C. Photographer

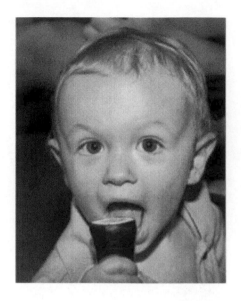

Image courtesy of chefranden

The answer is B. Musician

Musicians can play an instrument in an orchestra or band, or sing.

A baseball player is usually too busy playing baseball to have time to play a musical instrument.

Photographers like to take pictures.

Image courtesy of sermoa

What would you be if you built software for computers?

A. Programmer
B. Pharmacist
C. Candlestick Maker

Image courtesy of Scott & Elaine van der Chijs

The answer is A. Programmer

Programmers program computers so they will do what we want them to do.

Pharmacists keep busy making sure people get the right medicine.

Candlestick makers make candlesticks.

Image courtesy of Roberto Verzo

What would you be if you helped people know what to buy in a store?

A. Attorney
B. Salesperson
C. Waitress

Image courtesy of quinn anya

The answer is B. Salesperson

Salespeople can also sell things that aren't in stores.

Attorneys help people but not usually in a store.

Waitresses can help people decide what to order in a restaurant.

Image courtesy of amslerPIX

What would you be if you drove a big vehicle filled with people?

A. Bus Driver
B. Dentist
C. Truck Driver

Image courtesy of woodleywonderworks

The answer is A. Bus Driver

Bus drivers can drive for schools, cities or throughout the United States.

Dentists help to keep people's teeth healthy.

Truck drivers drive a big vehicle, but it isn't filled with people.

Image courtesy of Unique Hotels Group

What would you be if you made special dishes in a restaurant?

A. Chef
B. Interpreter
C. Scientist

Image courtesy of N A I T

The answer is A. Chef

Chefs spend a lot of time making sure the flavor of the food they make is exactly how they want it to be.

Interpreters can help translate different languages or communicate with deaf people.

Scientists study science to explore things through microscopes or telescopes.

Image courtesy of San Jose Library

What would you be if you wrote books or stories?

A. Author
B. Librarian
C. Musician

Image courtesy of San Jose Library

The answer is A. Author

Authors write stories for people from babies to adults, from short articles to thick books.

Librarians keep books organized so people can find the book they are looking for.

Musicians write music more than they write books.

Image courtesy of Joaquin Martinez Rosado

What would you be if you designed houses or tall buildings?

A. Architect
B. Basketball player
C. Surveyor

Image courtesy of Serge Melki

The answer is A. Architect

Without an architect, we couldn't have tall buildings that are safe to be in.

Basketball players may need tall buildings, but they don't design them!

Building designers sometimes need surveyors to determine the best place to put a building.

Image courtesy of Images of Money

What would you be if you helped people buy or sell houses?

A. Coach
B. Mechanic
C. Realtor

Image courtesy of Realtor Action Center

The answer is C. Realtor.

Realtors help make a complicated process easier for everybody.

Coaches help players play a better game, or they can help a business person have a better business.

Mechanics fix things including cars and trucks.

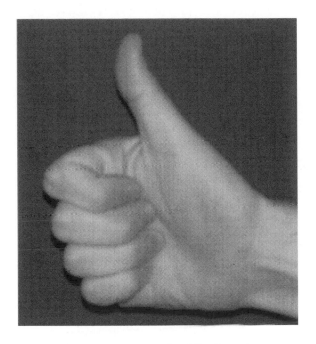

Image courtesy of public domain

Congratulations! You made it to the end!

Check out more fun books listed on the next pages.

A Horse of Course

Ballpark Facts for Fun! American League

Ballpark Facts for Fun! National League

Baseball Teams Facts for Fun! National League - Book 1

Baseball Teams Facts for Fun! National League - Book 2

Bible Book Facts for Fun! Old Testament

Bible Character Facts for Fun! New Testament

Bible Character Facts for Fun! Old Testament

Christmas Facts for Fun!

Dog Breed Facts for Fun! Airedales to Bull Terriers

Dog Breed Facts for Fun! Book A

Dog Breed Facts for Fun! Book B

Dog Breed Facts for Fun! Book C-D

Dog Breed Facts for Fun! Book E-I

Dog Breed Facts for Fun! Book J-M

Dog Breed Facts for Fun! Book O-R

Dog Breed Facts for Fun! Book S

Dog Breed Facts for Fun! Book W-Y

Easter Facts for Fun!

Farm Animal Facts for Fun!

First Letters for Fun! A-L

First Letters for Fun! M-Z

Football Player Facts for Fun! Quarterbacks

Football Player Facts for Fun! Wide Receivers

Horse Facts for Fun!

Nifty Fifty State Facts for Fun! Book 1

Nifty Fifty State Facts for Fun! Book 2

Presidential Facts for Fun! Washington to Polk

Presidential Facts for Fun! Taylor to Cleveland

Presidential Facts for Fun! Harrison to Truman

State Facts for Fun! California

State Facts for Fun! Colorado

State Facts for Fun! Florida